Josh and S

MW01713363

Rigby®
A Harcourt Achieve Imprint

www.Rigby.com
1-800-531-5015

Here comes Scruffy.

Look at Scruffy.

Look at Scruffy.

Scruffy is in the truck.

Look at Scruffy.

Scruffy is on the road.

Look at Scruffy.

Scruffy is in the box.

Look at Scruffy.

Scruffy is on the blocks.

"Come here, Scruffy.
Come here!"
said Josh.

Here comes Scruffy!